20 best gluten-free bread recipes

Houghton Mifflin Harcourt
Boston • New York • 2013

Copyright © 2013 by General Mills, Minneapolis, Minnesota. All rights reserved.

For information about permission to reproduce selections from this book, write to Permissions, Houghton Mifflin Harcourt Publishing Company, 215 Park Avenue South, New York, New York 10003.

www.hmhco.com

Cover photo: Best-Ever Banana Bread (page 17)

General Mills
Food Content and Relationship Marketing Director: Geoff Johnson
Food Content Marketing Manager: Susan Klobuchar
Senior Editor: Grace Wells
Kitchen Manager: Ann Stuart
Recipe Development and Testing: Betty Crocker Kitchens
Photography: General Mills Photography Studios and Image Library

Houghton Mifflin Harcourt
Publisher: Natalie Chapman
Editorial Director: Cindy Kitchel
Executive Editor: Anne Ficklen
Associate Editor: Heather Dabah
Managing Editor: Rebecca Springer
Production Editor: Kristi Hart
Cover Design: Chrissy Kurpeski
Book Design: Tai Blanche

ISBN 978-0-544-31480-1
Printed in the United States of America

The Betty Crocker Kitchens seal guarantees success in your kitchen. Every recipe has been tested in America's Most Trusted Kitchens™ to meet our high standards of reliability, easy preparation and great taste.

FIND MORE GREAT IDEAS AT
BettyCrocker.com

Dear Friends,

This new collection of colorful mini books has been put together with you in mind because we know that you love great recipes and enjoy cooking and baking but have a busy lifestyle. So every little book in the series contains just 20 recipes for you to treasure and enjoy. Plus, each book is a single subject designed in a bite-size format just for you—it's easy to use and is filled with favorite recipes from the Betty Crocker Kitchens!

All of the books are conveniently divided into short chapters so you can quickly find what you're looking for, and the beautiful photos throughout are sure to entice you into making the delicious recipes. In the series, you'll discover a fabulous array of recipes to spark your interest—from cookies, cupcakes and birthday cakes to party ideas for a variety of occasions. There's grilled foods, potluck favorites and even gluten-free recipes too.

You'll love the variety in these mini books—so pick one or choose them all for your cooking pleasure.

Enjoy and happy cooking!

Sincerely,

Betty Crocker

contents

Coffee Cakes and Scones
Fruit Swirl Coffee Cake · 6
Cinnamon-Streusel Coffee Cake · 7
Eggnog Breakfast Cake · 8
Decadent Chocolate Chip Scones · 9
Strawberries-and-Cream Scones · 10
Cinnamon Scones · 11

Muffins and Loaves
Banana–Chocolate Chip Muffins · 12
Apricot Muffins with Almond-Streusel Topping · 13
Strawberry Muffins · 14
Caramel-Pecan Upside-Down Muffins · 15
Blueberry Corn Muffins · 16
Best-Ever Banana Bread · 17
Pumpkin Bread · 18

Savory Favorites
Biscuits · 19
Cheese-Garlic Biscuits · 20
"A-Maize-ing" Cornbread · 21
Sandwich Bread · 22
Sesame Seed Hamburger Buns · 23
Dinner Rolls · 24
Soft Pretzels · 25

Metric Conversion Guide · 26
Recipe Testing and Calculating Nutrition Information · 27

Coffee Cakes and Scones

Fruit Swirl Coffee Cake

Prep Time: 20 Minutes • **Start to Finish:** 45 Minutes • Makes 18 servings

Coffee Cake

- 4 eggs
- ¾ cup milk
- ½ cup butter, melted
- 2 teaspoons gluten-free vanilla
- 1 box Bisquick® Gluten Free mix (3 cups)
- ⅔ cup granulated sugar
- 1 can (21 oz) gluten-free fruit pie filling (any flavor)

Glaze

- 1 cup gluten-free powdered sugar
- 2 tablespoons milk

1 Heat oven to 375°F. Grease 1 (15 x 10 x 1-inch) pan or 2 (9-inch) square pans with shortening or cooking spray (without flour).

2 In large bowl, stir all coffee cake ingredients except pie filling until blended; beat vigorously 30 seconds. Spread two-thirds of the batter (about 2½ cups) in 15 x 10 x 1-inch pan or one-third of the batter (about 1¼ cups) in each square pan.

3 Spread pie filling over batter (filling may not cover batter completely). Drop remaining batter by tablespoonfuls onto pie filling.

4 Bake 20 to 25 minutes or until golden brown. Meanwhile, in small bowl, mix all glaze ingredients until smooth. Drizzle glaze over warm coffee cake. Serve warm or cool.

1 Serving: Calories 240; Total Fat 7g (Saturated Fat 4g, Trans Fat 0g); Cholesterol 60mg; Sodium 280mg; Total Carbohydrate 41g (Dietary Fiber 0g); Protein 3g **Exchanges:** 1 Starch, 1½ Other Carbohydrate, 1½ Fat **Carbohydrate Choices:** 3

Tip This easy fruit-filled coffee cake is ripe for any flavor of filling—take your pick! Try apple, cherry, blueberry, peach or apricot pie filling. Or try gluten-free lemon curd for a luscious citrus twist.

Cinnamon-Streusel Coffee Cake

Prep Time: 10 Minutes • **Start to Finish:** 40 Minutes • Makes 6 servings

Topping

- ⅓ cup Bisquick Gluten Free mix
- ½ cup packed brown sugar
- ¾ teaspoon ground cinnamon
- ¼ cup cold butter or margarine

Coffee Cake

- 1¾ cups Bisquick Gluten Free mix
- 3 tablespoons granulated sugar
- ⅔ cup milk or water
- 1½ teaspoons gluten-free vanilla
- 3 eggs

1 Heat oven to 350°F. Spray 9-inch round or square pan with cooking spray.

2 In small bowl, mix ⅓ cup Bisquick mix, the brown sugar and cinnamon. Cut in butter, using pastry blender or fork, until mixture is crumbly.

3 In medium bowl, stir all coffee cake ingredients until blended. Spread in pan; sprinkle with topping.

4 Bake 25 to 30 minutes or until golden brown. Store tightly covered.

1 Serving: Calories 360; Total Fat 11g (Saturated Fat 6g, Trans Fat 0g); Cholesterol 130mg; Sodium 460mg; Total Carbohydrate 58g (Dietary Fiber 1g); Protein 6g **Exchanges:** 2½ Starch, 1½ Other Carbohydrate, 2 Fat **Carbohydrate Choices:** 4

Eggnog Breakfast Cake

Prep Time: 15 Minutes • **Start to Finish:** 1 Hour 40 Minutes • Makes 9 servings

- 1 box Betty Crocker® Gluten Free yellow cake mix
- ⅔ cup milk
- ½ cup butter, softened
- 1½ teaspoons gluten-free rum extract
- 1 teaspoon gluten-free vanilla
- ¼ teaspoon ground nutmeg
- 3 eggs
- ¼ cup Betty Crocker Rich & Creamy vanilla frosting (from 1-lb container)
- ⅓ cup chopped pecans

1 Heat oven to 350°F (325°F for dark or nonstick pan). Grease bottom only of 8- or 9-inch square or round cake pan with shortening or cooking spray (without flour).

2 In large bowl, beat cake mix, milk, butter, rum extract, vanilla, nutmeg and eggs with electric mixer on low speed 30 seconds, then on medium speed 2 minutes, scraping bowl occasionally. Pour into pan.

3 Bake 33 to 41 minutes or until toothpick inserted in center comes out clean. Cool 10 minutes. Run knife around inside edge of pan. Cool 30 minutes longer.

4 In small microwavable bowl, microwave frosting uncovered on High 10 to 15 seconds or until easy to drizzle. Drizzle frosting over cake; sprinkle with pecans.

1 Serving: Calories 320; Total Fat 15g (Saturated Fat 7g, Trans Fat 1g); Cholesterol 90mg; Sodium 330mg; Total Carbohydrate 43g (Dietary Fiber 0g); Protein 4g **Exchanges:** 1 Starch, 2 Other Carbohydrate, 3 Fat **Carbohydrate Choices:** 3

Tip For an indulgent treat, use candied pecans. They're available with the other nuts or in the snacking section of the grocery store—just make sure they're gluten free.

Decadent Chocolate Chip Scones

Prep Time: 20 Minutes • **Start to Finish:** 40 Minutes • Makes 12 scones

2 cups Bisquick Gluten Free mix

1 cup semisweet chocolate chips (6 oz)

1⅓ cups whipping cream

½ teaspoon gluten-free almond extract

1 cup powdered sugar

2 to 3 tablespoons milk or water

3 tablespoons sliced almonds

1 Heat oven to 400°F. Line cookie sheet with cooking parchment paper.

2 In large bowl, stir Bisquick mix and chocolate chips until mixed. In small bowl, mix whipping cream and ¼ teaspoon of the almond extract. Stir into Bisquick mixture until soft dough forms, adding 1 to 2 tablespoons additional whipping cream if necessary.

3 Divide dough in half. On surface sprinkled with Bisquick Gluten Free mix, pat each half into 6-inch round. Cut each round into 6 wedges. Place wedges about 2 inches apart on cookie sheet.

4 Bake 10 to 13 minutes or until golden brown. Cool 5 minutes. Remove parchment paper with scones to cooling rack. In small bowl, mix powdered sugar, remaining ¼ teaspoon almond extract and enough milk for desired drizzling consistency. Drizzle half of the icing over warm scones. Sprinkle with almonds. Drizzle with remaining icing. Serve warm.

1 Scone: Calories 280; Total Fat 13g (Saturated Fat 8g, Trans Fat 0g); Cholesterol 30mg; Sodium 240mg; Total Carbohydrate 37g (Dietary Fiber 1g); Protein 2g **Exchanges:** 1 Starch, 1½ Other Carbohydrate, 2½ Fat **Carbohydrate Choices:** 2½

Strawberries-and-Cream Scones

Prep Time: 20 Minutes • **Start to Finish:** 50 Minutes • Makes 10 scones

- 1 cup white rice flour
- ½ cup tapioca flour
- ¼ cup millet flour
- ¼ cup potato starch
- 2 teaspoons xanthan gum
- 3 tablespoons sugar
- 1 tablespoon gluten-free baking powder
- ½ teaspoon salt
- 6 tablespoons cold unsalted butter, cut into ¼-inch pieces
- ½ cup chopped fresh strawberries
- 1¼ cups whipping cream

1 Heat oven to 375°F. Line cookie sheet with cooking parchment paper.

2 In large bowl, mix all flours, the potato starch, xanthan gum, 2 tablespoons of the sugar, the baking powder and salt with whisk. Cut in butter, using pastry blender or fork, until coarse crumbs form. Add strawberries; stir gently to coat with crumb mixture. Stir in 1 cup plus 2 tablespoons of the whipping cream, mixing just until combined.

3 Onto cookie sheet, drop dough by ¼ cupfuls about 2 inches apart. Brush with remaining 2 tablespoons whipping cream; sprinkle with remaining 1 tablespoon sugar.

4 Bake 25 to 30 minutes or until golden and puffed. Remove from cookie sheet to cooling rack. Serve warm.

1 Scone: Calories 280; Total Fat 17g (Saturated Fat 10g, Trans Fat 0.5g); Cholesterol 50mg; Sodium 280mg; Total Carbohydrate 29g (Dietary Fiber 1g); Protein 2g **Exchanges:** 1 Starch, 1 Other Carbohydrate, 3 Fat **Carbohydrate Choices:** 2

Contributed by Silvana Nardone
Silvana's Kitchen www.silvanaskitchen.com

Tip If you can't find millet flour at your local supermarket, increase the white rice flour to 1¼ cups.

Cinnamon Scones

Prep Time: 10 Minutes • **Start to Finish:** 30 Minutes • Makes 8 scones

Scones

- ⅔ cup tapioca flour
- ⅔ cup white rice flour
- 1 cup potato starch
- 6 tablespoons sugar
- 4 teaspoons gluten-free baking powder
- 1 teaspoon baking soda
- 1 teaspoon ground cinnamon
- ½ teaspoon salt
- 2 eggs
- ⅔ cup melted ghee or coconut oil
- ¼ cup gluten-free almond milk, rice milk, soymilk or regular milk
- 1 teaspoon xanthan gum
- 1 teaspoon guar gum

Topping

- 2 tablespoons sugar
- 1 teaspoon ground cinnamon

1 Heat oven to 400°F. Line cookie sheet with cooking parchment paper; spray paper with cooking spray (without flour). In medium bowl, mix all flours, the potato starch, 6 tablespoons sugar, the baking powder, baking soda, 1 teaspoon cinnamon and the salt.

2 In small bowl, beat eggs, melted ghee, milk and both gums with electric mixer until well blended. Add egg mixture to flour mixture; beat with electric mixer on low speed until blended.

3 Coat work surface and hands with oil. Place dough on surface; pat into round, about 1 inch thick. Cut dough round into 8 wedges; place about 1 inch apart on cookie sheet. In small bowl, mix all topping ingredients; sprinkle over dough.

4 Bake 14 to 18 minutes or until set. Remove from cookie sheet to cooling rack. Serve warm.

1 Scone: Calories 400; Total Fat 20g (Saturated Fat 16g, Trans Fat 0g); Cholesterol 55mg; Sodium 570mg; Total Carbohydrate 54g (Dietary Fiber 1g); Protein 2g **Exchanges:** 1½ Starch, 1 Fruit, 1 Other Carbohydrate 3½ Fat **Carbohydrate Choices:** 3½

Contributed by Jean Duane Alternative Cook
www.alternativecook.com

Chocolate Scones:
Omit the cinnamon-sugar topping and stir ¼ cup miniature chocolate chips into the batter.

Muffins and Loaves

Banana-Chocolate Chip Muffins

Prep Time: 20 Minutes • **Start to Finish:** 45 Minutes • Makes 16 muffins

½ cup finely ground tapioca flour
½ cup white rice flour
¼ cup garbanzo and fava flour
¼ cup sweet white sorghum flour
½ cup potato starch
½ teaspoon xanthan gum
1 teaspoon gluten-free baking powder
1 teaspoon baking soda
½ teaspoon salt
2 eggs
½ cup sunflower or canola oil or ghee (measured melted)
¼ cup almond milk, soymilk or regular milk
1 cup mashed ripe bananas (2 medium)
⅔ cup packed brown sugar
2 teaspoons gluten-free vanilla
½ cup miniature semisweet chocolate chips

1 Heat oven to 350°F. Spray 16 regular-size muffin cups with cooking spray (without flour).

2 In small bowl, mix all flours, the potato starch, xanthan gum, baking powder, baking soda and salt with whisk; set aside. In medium bowl, beat eggs, oil, milk, bananas, brown sugar and vanilla with electric mixer on medium speed until well blended. Gradually add flour mixture, beating until well blended. Stir in chocolate chips. Divide batter evenly among muffin cups, filling each about three-fourths full.

3 Bake 18 to 20 minutes or until toothpick inserted in center comes out clean. Cool 5 minutes. Remove from pans to cooling racks. Serve warm.

1 Muffin: Calories 220; Total Fat 9g (Saturated Fat 2g, Trans Fat 0g); Cholesterol 25mg; Sodium 200mg; Total Carbohydrate 30g (Dietary Fiber 2g); Protein 2g **Exchanges:** 1 Starch, 1 Other Carbohydrate, 1½ Fat **Carbohydrate Choices:** 2

Banana-Date Muffins:
Substitute chopped dates (don't toss with flour) for the chocolate chips; add ½ cup chopped nuts and 1 teaspoon ground cinnamon.

Tip This recipe is a great way to use bananas that are getting a little too ripe. You may find you buy bananas just to make these muffins!

Apricot Muffins with Almond-Streusel Topping

Prep Time: 25 Minutes • **Start to Finish:** 1 Hour 5 Minutes • Makes 14 muffins

Muffins

- ½ cup sorghum flour
- ½ cup tapioca flour
- ½ cup white rice flour
- ¼ cup garbanzo and fava flour
- ¼ cup potato starch
- 1 teaspoon gluten-free baking powder
- 1 teaspoon baking soda
- 1 teaspoon xanthan gum
- ½ teaspoon salt
- 2 eggs
- 1 cup gluten-free almond milk, rice milk, soymilk or regular milk
- ½ cup sunflower oil or melted ghee
- ½ cup granulated sugar
- 1 teaspoon apple cider vinegar
- 1 teaspoon gluten-free vanilla
- ½ cup chopped dried apricots

Topping

- ¼ cup melted ghee
- ½ cup packed brown sugar
- ½ cup slivered almonds, toasted*

1 Heat oven to 400°F. Place paper baking cup in each of 14 regular-size muffin cups; spray paper cups with cooking spray (without flour). In small bowl, stir all flours, the potato starch, baking powder, baking soda, xanthan gum and salt; set aside.

2 In medium bowl, beat eggs, milk, oil, granulated sugar, vinegar and vanilla until well blended. Add flour mixture; stir until dry ingredients are moistened. Stir in apricots. Divide batter evenly among muffin cups, filling each until batter is ½ inch from top of paper baking cup.

3 In another small bowl, mix all topping ingredients until crumbly. Sprinkle evenly over batter in cups.

4 Bake 25 to 30 minutes or until tops of muffins spring back when touched lightly in center. Cool 10 minutes. Remove from pans to cooling racks. Carefully remove paper baking cups.

*To toast almonds, spread in ungreased shallow pan. Bake uncovered at 350°F 6 to 10 minutes, stirring occasionally, until light brown.

1 Muffin: Calories 300; Total Fat 15g (Saturated Fat 4g, Trans Fat 0g); Cholesterol 40mg; Sodium 230mg; Total Carbohydrate 35g (Dietary Fiber 1g); Protein 3g **Exchanges:** ½ Starch, 1 Fruit, 1 Other Carbohydrate, 3 Fat **Carbohydrate Choices:** 2

Contributed by Jean Duane Alternative Cook
www.alternativecook.com

Tip If you're substituting milk, try to find substitutes with the same fat content. Unsweetened almond or hemp seed milk works beautifully in baked recipes as a dairy substitute. Both are available at natural grocery stores.

Strawberry Muffins

Prep Time: 10 Minutes • **Start to Finish:** 35 Minutes • Makes 10 muffins

- 1¼ cups Bisquick Gluten Free mix
- ½ cup packed light brown sugar
- 6 tablespoons fat-free (skim) milk
- 3 tablespoons butter, melted
- 3 teaspoons gluten-free vanilla
- 1 egg
- ¼ cup diced fresh strawberries
- 1 teaspoon Bisquick Gluten Free mix
- 10 fresh strawberry slices

1 Heat oven to 375°F. Place paper baking cup in each of 10 regular-size muffin cups.

2 In medium bowl, stir 1¼ cups Bisquick mix and the brown sugar with whisk. Make well in center of mixture. In small bowl, stir milk, butter, vanilla and egg with whisk until well blended. Add to Bisquick mixture, stirring just until moistened. In small bowl, lightly toss diced strawberries and 1 teaspoon Bisquick mix. Stir into batter. Divide batter evenly among muffin cups.

3 Bake 10 minutes. Place 1 strawberry slice on top of each muffin. Bake 8 minutes longer or until lightly browned. Cool 5 minutes. Remove from pan to cooling rack. Serve warm.

1 Muffin: Calories 127; Total Fat 5g (Saturated Fat 2g, Trans Fat 0g); Cholesterol 0mg; Sodium 158mg; Total Carbohydrate 19g (Dietary Fiber 1g); Protein 3g **Exchanges:** ½ Starch, ½ Other Carbohydrate, 1 Fat **Carbohydrate Choices:** 1

Caramel-Pecan Upside-Down Muffins

Prep Time: 15 Minutes • **Start to Finish:** 35 Minutes • Makes 12 muffins

6 tablespoons butter or margarine, melted
¼ cup packed brown sugar
½ cup chopped pecans
1⅓ cups Bisquick Gluten Free mix
⅓ cup granulated sugar
¼ cup butter, melted
½ cup milk
3 eggs, beaten
½ teaspoon ground cinnamon

1 Heat oven to 400°F. Spray 12 regular-size muffin cups with cooking spray (without flour).

2 In small bowl, mix 6 tablespoons butter, the brown sugar and pecans. Divide mixture evenly among muffin cups. In medium bowl, stir remaining ingredients until soft dough forms. Drop spoonfuls of dough into each muffin cup.

3 Bake 12 to 14 minutes or until toothpick inserted in center comes out clean. Turn pan upside down onto cookie sheet; leave pan over muffins 2 to 3 minutes to allow brown sugar mixture to drizzle over muffins. Remove pan; replace any topping left in pan on muffin tops. Serve warm.

1 Muffin: Calories 230; Total Fat 14g (Saturated Fat 7g, Trans Fat 0g); Cholesterol 80mg; Sodium 240mg; Total Carbohydrate 23g (Dietary Fiber 0g); Protein 3g **Exchanges:** ½ Starch, 1 Other Carbohydrate, 3 Fat **Carbohydrate Choices:** 1½

Caramel-Almond Upside-Down Muffins: Substitute sliced almonds for the pecans.

Tip Serve with your favorite fresh fruit such as sliced cantaloupe, strawberries or pineapple chunks.

Muffins and Loaves

Blueberry Corn Muffins

Prep Time: 10 Minutes • **Start to Finish:** 30 Minutes • Makes 18 muffins

- 1 box Betty Crocker Gluten Free yellow cake mix
- ½ cup yellow cornmeal
- ¾ cup water
- ½ cup butter, melted
- 2 teaspoons gluten-free vanilla
- 3 eggs, beaten
- 2 teaspoons grated orange peel
- 1½ cups fresh or frozen (do not thaw) blueberries
- 1 tablespoon sugar

1 Heat oven to 375°F. Place 1 paper baking cup in each of 18 regular-size muffin cups.

2 In large bowl, mix cake mix, cornmeal, water, butter, vanilla, eggs and orange peel just until dry ingredients are moistened. Gently stir in blueberries. Divide batter evenly among muffin cups. Sprinkle with sugar.

3 Bake 15 to 20 minutes or until toothpick inserted in center comes out clean. Immediately remove from pans to cooling racks. Serve warm or cool.

1 Muffin: Calories 170; Total Fat 6g (Saturated Fat 3.5g, Trans Fat 0g); Cholesterol 50mg; Sodium 170mg; Total Carbohydrate 27g (Dietary Fiber 0g); Protein 2g **Exchanges:** ½ Starch, 1½ Other Carbohydrate, 1 Fat **Carbohydrate Choices:** 2

Tip These not-too-sweet muffins would be awesome with orange butter. Stir grated orange peel into softened butter and you've got it!

Best-Ever Banana Bread

Prep Time: 10 Minutes • **Start to Finish:** 2 Hours 15 Minutes • Makes 1 loaf (16 slices)

- ½ cup tapioca flour
- ½ cup white rice flour
- ¼ cup garbanzo and fava flour
- ¼ cup sorghum flour
- ½ cup potato starch
- 1 teaspoon xanthan gum
- ½ teaspoon guar gum
- 1 teaspoon gluten-free baking powder
- 1 teaspoon baking soda
- 1 teaspoon ground cinnamon
- 1 teaspoon salt
- ¾ cup packed brown sugar
- 1 cup mashed very ripe bananas (2 medium)
- ½ cup melted ghee
- ¼ cup gluten-free almond milk, rice milk, soymilk or regular milk
- 1 teaspoon gluten-free vanilla
- 2 eggs

1 Heat oven to 350°F. Generously spray bottom and sides of 9 x 5-inch loaf pan with cooking spray (without flour). In small bowl, stir all flours, the potato starch, both gums, baking powder, baking soda, cinnamon and salt; set aside.

2 In medium bowl, beat remaining ingredients with whisk until blended. Add flour mixture; stir until thoroughly mixed. Pour into pan.

3 Bake 30 minutes. Cover with foil; bake 25 to 30 minutes longer or until toothpick inserted in center comes out almost clean. Cool 5 minutes. Remove loaf from pan; place on cooling rack. Cool completely, about 1 hour. Wrap tightly and store in refrigerator.

1 Slice: Calories 200; Total Fat 9g (Saturated Fat 5g, Trans Fat 0g); Cholesterol 40mg; Sodium 270mg; Total Carbohydrate 29g (Dietary Fiber 1g); Protein 2g **Exchanges:** 1 Starch, ½ Fruit, ½ Other Carbohydrate, 1½ Fat **Carbohydrate Choices:** 2

Contributed by Jean Duane Alternative Cook
www.alternativecook.com

Apple Bread: Substitute applesauce for the mashed bananas.

Pumpkin Bread

Prep Time: 10 Minutes • **Start to Finish:** 3 Hours 25 Minutes • Makes 16 servings

- 1 box Betty Crocker Gluten Free yellow cake mix
- 1 can (15 oz) pumpkin (not pumpkin pie mix)
- ½ cup canola oil
- 1 teaspoon ground cinnamon
- ½ teaspoon ground ginger
- ¼ teaspoon ground cloves
- 2 teaspoons gluten-free vanilla
- ½ cup gluten-free semisweet chocolate chips (dairy- and nut-free)

1. Heat oven to 350°F. Grease bottom only of 9 x 5-inch or 8 x 4-inch loaf pan with oil.

2. In large bowl, stir all ingredients except chocolate chips until well mixed. Stir in chocolate chips. Spread evenly in pan.

3. Bake 9-inch loaf 55 to 65 minutes, 8-inch loaf 60 to 70 minutes, or until toothpick inserted in center comes out clean. Cool 10 minutes. Remove loaf from pan; place on cooling rack. Cool about 2 hours before slicing.

1 Serving: Calories 200; Total Fat 8g (Saturated Fat 1.5g, Trans Fat 0g); Cholesterol 0mg; Sodium 150mg; Total Carbohydrate 29g (Dietary Fiber 1g); Protein 1g **Exchanges:** ½ Starch, 1½ Other Carbohydrate, 1½ Fat **Carbohydrate Choices:** 2

Tip Always read labels to make sure each ingredient is free of allergens that you are sensitive to. Products and ingredient sources can change.

Savory Favorites

Biscuits

Prep Time: 10 Minutes • **Start to Finish:** 30 Minutes • Makes 10 biscuits

2 cups Bisquick Gluten Free mix
⅓ cup shortening
⅔ cup milk
3 eggs

1 Heat oven to 400°F. Place Bisquick mix in large bowl. Cut in shortening, using pastry blender or fork, until mixture looks like coarse crumbs. Stir in remaining ingredients until soft dough forms.

2 Onto ungreased cookie sheet, drop dough by rounded tablespoonfuls about 3 inches apart.

3 Bake 13 to 16 minutes or until golden brown.

1 Biscuit: Calories 180; Total Fat 9g (Saturated Fat 2.5g, Trans Fat 1g); Cholesterol 65mg; Sodium 300mg; Total Carbohydrate 21g (Dietary Fiber 0g); Protein 3g **Exchanges:** 1½ Starch, 1½ Fat **Carbohydrate Choices:** 1½

Tip Top warm biscuits with your favorite jelly, jam or honey.

Cheese-Garlic Biscuits

Prep Time: 5 Minutes • **Start to Finish:** 15 Minutes • Makes 10 biscuits

Biscuits

2 cups Bisquick Gluten Free mix

¼ teaspoon garlic powder

¼ cup cold butter or margarine

⅔ cup milk

½ cup shredded Cheddar cheese (2 oz)

3 eggs

Topping

¼ cup butter or margarine, melted

¼ teaspoon garlic powder

1 Heat oven to 425°F. In medium bowl, stir together Bisquick mix and ¼ teaspoon garlic powder. Cut in ¼ cup butter, using pastry blender or fork, until mixture looks like coarse crumbs. Stir in milk, cheese and eggs until soft dough forms.

2 Onto ungreased cookie sheet, drop dough by 10 spoonfuls.

3 Bake 8 to 10 minutes or until light golden brown. In small bowl, mix ¼ cup melted butter and ¼ teaspoon garlic powder; brush on warm biscuits before removing from cookie sheet. Serve warm.

1 Biscuit: Calories 230; Total Fat 13g (Saturated Fat 8g, Trans Fat 0g); Cholesterol 95mg; Sodium 400mg; Total Carbohydrate 22g (Dietary Fiber 0g); Protein 5g **Exchanges:** 1½ Starch, 2½ Fat **Carbohydrate Choices:** 1½

Tip Add about 1 tablespoon finely chopped fresh parsley to the Bisquick mix and garlic powder to add a little color to these biscuits.

"A-Maize-ing" Cornbread

Prep Time: 15 Minutes • **Start to Finish:** 55 Minutes • Makes 18 servings

- 1⅓ cups plus 1 tablespoon gluten-free cornmeal
- 1 box Betty Crocker Gluten Free yellow cake mix
- 1 tablespoon sugar
- ½ teaspoon baking soda
- 1⅓ cups gluten-free sour cream
- ½ cup vegetable oil
- 3 eggs, beaten
- 1 lb gluten-free ground pork sausage, cooked, drained
- 1 cup gluten-free shredded Cheddar cheese (4 oz)
- 1 jalapeño chile, seeded, finely chopped (about 5 teaspoons)

1 Heat oven to 350°F. Grease 13 x 9-inch pan. Sprinkle pan with 1 tablespoon of the cornmeal.

2 In large bowl, mix cake mix, 1⅓ cups cornmeal, the sugar and baking soda; mix well.

3 In small bowl, mix sour cream, oil and eggs. Add to cornmeal mixture; mix well. Fold in sausage, cheese and jalapeño chile. Spread in pan.

4 Bake 35 to 40 minutes or until toothpick inserted in center comes out clean. Serve warm.

1 Serving: Calories 340; Total Fat 20g (Saturated Fat 7g, Trans Fat 0g); Cholesterol 70mg; Sodium 420mg; Total Carbohydrate 32g (Dietary Fiber 0g); Protein 9g **Exchanges:** ½ Starch, 1½ Other Carbohydrate, 1 Medium-Fat Meat, 3 Fat **Carbohydrate Choices:** 2

Sandwich Bread

Prep Time: 30 Minutes • **Start to Finish:** 3 Hours 45 Minutes • Makes 1 loaf (16 slices)

- ¾ cup warm water (105°F to 115°F)
- 1 tablespoon fast-acting dry yeast
- ¾ cup plus 1 tablespoon tapioca flour
- ½ cup white rice flour
- ¼ cup garbanzo and fava flour
- ¼ cup sweet white sorghum flour
- ½ cup plus 2 tablespoons potato starch
- 1½ teaspoons salt
- 1½ teaspoons gluten-free baking powder
- 1 teaspoon xanthan gum
- 2 eggs
- ¼ cup sugar
- ¼ cup sunflower oil
- 1 teaspoon guar gum
- ½ teaspoon apple cider vinegar
- Cooking spray (without flour)

1 Spray bottom and sides of 8 x 4-inch loaf pan with cooking spray (without flour). In small bowl, stir water and yeast until dissolved; set aside.

2 In another small bowl, stir all flours, the potato starch, salt, baking powder and xanthan gum; set aside.

3 In medium bowl, beat all remaining ingredients except cooking spray with electric mixer on medium speed 1 to 2 minutes. Beat in yeast mixture. Add flour mixture; beat on medium speed until thoroughly mixed. Pour into pan. Spray top of dough with cooking spray; if necessary, smooth top of dough with spatula. Cover with plastic wrap; let rise in warm place (80°F to 85°F) 1 hour to 1 hour 30 minutes or until dough rises to top of pan.

4 Heat oven to 375°F. Carefully remove plastic wrap from pan; bake 30 minutes. Reduce oven temperature to 350°F. Cover loaf with cooking parchment paper; bake 25 to 30 minutes longer or until instant-read thermometer inserted in center of loaf reads 207°F. Cool 5 minutes. Remove loaf from pan; place on cooling rack. Cool completely, about 40 minutes.

1 Slice: Calories 140; Total Fat 4.5g (Saturated Fat 0.5g, Trans Fat 0g); Cholesterol 25mg; Sodium 280mg; Total Carbohydrate 22g (Dietary Fiber 1g); Protein 2g **Exchanges:** 1 Starch, ½ Other Carbohydrate, 1 Fat **Carbohydrate Choices:** 1½

Contributed by Jean Duane Alternative Cook
www.alternativecook.com

Tip Gluten-free bread looks "done" long before it is done, so don't be afraid to bake it for an hour.

Sesame Seed Hamburger Buns

Prep Time: 25 Minutes • **Start to Finish:** 3 Hours 15 Minutes • Makes 6 buns

- 1 tablespoon fast-acting dry yeast
- ¾ cup warm water (105°F to 115°F)
- ¾ cup plus 1 tablespoon finely ground tapioca flour
- ½ cup white rice flour
- ¼ cup garbanzo and fava flour
- ¼ cup sweet white sorghum flour
- 1½ teaspoons xanthan gum
- 1 teaspoon guar gum
- ½ cup plus 2 tablespoons cornstarch
- 1¾ teaspoons salt
- 1½ teaspoons gluten-free baking powder
- 2 eggs
- ⅓ cup sugar
- ¼ cup sunflower oil
- ½ teaspoon cider vinegar
- 1 tablespoon sesame seed
- 1 egg white, beaten

1 Line cookie sheet with cooking parchment paper; spray paper with cooking spray (without flour). In small bowl, stir water and yeast until dissolved; set aside.

2 In medium bowl, mix all flours, both gums, the cornstarch, salt and baking powder with whisk; set aside. In large bowl, beat eggs, sugar, oil and vinegar with electric mixer on medium speed. Beat in yeast mixture. Gradually add flour mixture, beating on medium speed until well blended (dough will be sticky).

3 Using ¼-cup measure, drop dough into 6 portions onto cookie sheet. With wet hands, shape into buns, about 3¼ x 2 inches. Cover with plastic wrap; let rise in warm place (80°F to 85°F) about 1 hour 30 minutes or until doubled in size.

4 Heat oven to 350°F. Spread sesame seed in ungreased shallow pan. Bake uncovered 8 to 10 minutes, stirring occasionally, until golden brown. Set aside to cool. Remove plastic wrap from buns. Brush egg white over tops, being careful not to punch them down; sprinkle with toasted sesame seed.

5 Increase oven temperature to 375°F. Bake buns 15 minutes. Reduce oven temperature to 350°F. Cover buns with cooking parchment paper; bake 5 minutes longer or until instant-read thermometer inserted in center reads 207°F. Remove from cookie sheet to cooling rack. Cool completely, about 1 hour. Split buns with serrated knife.

1 Bun: Calories 400; Total Fat 13g (Saturated Fat 1.5g, Trans Fat 0g); Cholesterol 70mg; Sodium 850mg; Total Carbohydrate 66g (Dietary Fiber 3g); Protein 6g **Exchanges:** 2½ Starch, 2 Other Carbohydrate, 2 Fat **Carbohydrate Choices:** 4½

Contributed by Jean Duane Alternative Cook
www.alternativecook.com

Tip Gluten-free bread dough is more like a batter and is very sticky. The floured surface commonly used with gluten-containing dough doesn't work with this type of dough. For best results, use wet hands to work with it and shape it.

Dinner Rolls

Prep Time: 30 Minutes • **Start to Finish:** 2 Hours 15 Minutes • Makes 24 rolls

- ½ cup warm water (105°F to 115°F)
- 1 teaspoon unflavored gelatin
- 2¼ teaspoons fast-rising dry yeast
- ½ cup sorghum flour
- ½ cup brown rice flour
- ½ cup white rice flour
- ⅓ cup garbanzo and fava flour
- ⅓ cup tapioca flour
- ¾ cup cornstarch
- ¾ cup potato starch
- 2 eggs
- ½ cup gluten-free almond milk, rice milk, soymilk or regular milk
- ¼ cup honey
- 3 tablespoons sunflower oil or melted ghee
- 1 teaspoon apple cider vinegar
- 2 teaspoons xanthan gum
- 1½ teaspoons salt

1 Spray 24 regular-size muffin cups with cooking spray (without flour). In small bowl, stir water, gelatin and yeast until dissolved; set aside. In medium bowl, stir all flours, the cornstarch and potato starch; set aside.

2 In food processor, place eggs, milk, honey, oil, vinegar, xanthan gum and salt. Process about 30 seconds or until well blended. Add flour mixture and yeast mixture; process about 30 seconds or until well blended.

3 Spray 2 teaspoons with cooking spray (without flour). Spoon 3 balls of dough into each muffin cup, re-spraying spoons as necessary. Spray sheet of plastic wrap with cooking spray (without flour); cover dough in pans. Let rise in warm place (80°F to 85°F) 1 hour to 1 hour 30 minutes or until doubled in size.

4 Heat oven to 375°F. Bake 14 to 16 minutes or until light golden brown. Immediately turn rolls out of pans onto cooling racks. Serve warm.

1 Roll: Calories 120; Total Fat 2.5g (Saturated Fat 0g, Trans Fat 0g); Cholesterol 20mg; Sodium 160mg; Total Carbohydrate 22g (Dietary Fiber 1g); Protein 2g **Exchanges:** 1½ Starch **Carbohydrate Choices:** 1½

Contributed by Jean Duane Alternative Cook
www.alternativecook.com

Tip Although these are fantastic right out of the oven, they can also be baked and frozen in an airtight container, then popped into the toaster oven when you're ready to serve them.

Soft Pretzels

Prep Time: 30 Minutes • **Start to Finish:** 2 Hours 15 Minutes • Makes 12 pretzels

Pretzels

- 4½ teaspoons regular active dry yeast
- ⅔ cup warm water (105°F to 115°F)
- 1 cup finely ground tapioca flour
- ⅔ cup sweet white sorghum flour
- ¼ cup garbanzo and fava flour
- 1 cup cornstarch
- 1½ teaspoons xanthan gum
- ½ teaspoon guar gum
- 1 teaspoon salt
- 3 eggs
- 1 tablespoon sugar
- 1 tablespoon honey
- Additional garbanzo and fava flour
- Cooking spray (without flour)

Soda Bath

- ⅔ cup baking soda
- 10 cups water

Topping

- 1 egg, beaten
- 1 tablespoon kosher (coarse) salt

1 Line cookie sheet with cooking parchment paper; spray paper with cooking spray (without flour). In small bowl, stir water and yeast until dissolved; set aside.

2 In small bowl, mix all flours, the cornstarch, both gums and 1 teaspoon salt with whisk; set aside. In medium bowl, beat 3 eggs, the sugar and honey with electric mixer on medium speed 1 minute or until well blended. Add yeast mixture and flour mixture; beat 1 minute or until blended.

3 Divide dough into 12 equal-size balls. On work surface sprinkled with additional garbanzo and fava flour, roll each ball into 13 x ¾-inch rope. Carefully place ropes on cookie sheet; form into U shape and twist in middle. Spray tops of pretzels with cooking spray (without flour). Cover with plastic wrap; let rise in warm place (80°F to 85°F) 1 hour to 1 hour 30 minutes or until doubled in size.

4 Heat oven to 375°F. In 4-quart saucepan or Dutch oven, stir baking soda into water until dissolved. Heat to full rolling boil. Carefully place 1 pretzel at a time in water; boil 25 seconds. Remove with slotted spoon and return to cookie sheet. Brush tops of pretzels with egg, being careful not to fill openings with egg; sprinkle with kosher salt.

5 Bake 12 to 15 minutes or until golden brown. Immediately remove from cookie sheet to cooling rack.

1 Pretzel: Calories 160; Total Fat 2g (Saturated Fat 0.5g, Trans Fat 0g); Cholesterol 70mg; Sodium 4140mg; Total Carbohydrate 30g (Dietary Fiber 2g); Protein 4g **Exchanges:** 2 Starch **Carbohydrate Choices:** 2

Contributed by Jean Duane Alternative Cook
www.alternativecook.com

Tip The xanthan gum combined with the guar gum makes a nicely textured baked item. If you don't have guar gum, add an extra ½ teaspoon of xanthan gum in this recipe.

Metric Conversion Guide

Volume

U.S. Units	Canadian Metric	Australian Metric
¼ teaspoon	1 mL	1 ml
½ teaspoon	2 mL	2 ml
1 teaspoon	5 mL	5 ml
1 tablespoon	15 mL	20 ml
¼ cup	50 mL	60 ml
⅓ cup	75 mL	80 ml
½ cup	125 mL	125 ml
⅔ cup	150 mL	170 ml
¾ cup	175 mL	190 ml
1 cup	250 mL	250 ml
1 quart	1 liter	1 liter
1½ quarts	1.5 liters	1.5 liters
2 quarts	2 liters	2 liters
2½ quarts	2.5 liters	2.5 liters
3 quarts	3 liters	3 liters
4 quarts	4 liters	4 liters

Weight

U.S. Units	Canadian Metric	Australian Metric
1 ounce	30 grams	30 grams
2 ounces	55 grams	60 grams
3 ounces	85 grams	90 grams
4 ounces (¼ pound)	115 grams	125 grams
8 ounces (½ pound)	225 grams	225 grams
16 ounces (1 pound)	455 grams	500 grams
1 pound	455 grams	0.5 kilogram

Note: The recipes in this cookbook have not been developed or tested using metric measures. When converting recipes to metric, some variations in quality may be noted.

Measurements

Inches	Centimeters
1	2.5
2	5.0
3	7.5
4	10.0
5	12.5
6	15.0
7	17.5
8	20.5
9	23.0
10	25.5
11	28.0
12	30.5
13	33.0

Temperatures

Fahrenheit	Celsius
32°	0°
212°	100°
250°	120°
275°	140°
300°	150°
325°	160°
350°	180°
375°	190°
400°	200°
425°	220°
450°	230°
475°	240°
500°	260°

Recipe Testing and Calculating Nutrition Information

Recipe Testing:

- Large eggs and 2% milk were used unless otherwise indicated.
- Fat-free, low-fat, low-sodium or lite products were not used unless indicated.
- No nonstick cookware and bakeware were used unless otherwise indicated. No dark-colored, black or insulated bakeware was used.
- When a pan is specified, a metal pan was used; a baking dish or pie plate means ovenproof glass was used.
- An electric hand mixer was used for mixing only when mixer speeds are specified.

Calculating Nutrition:

- The first ingredient was used wherever a choice is given, such as ⅓ cup sour cream or plain yogurt.
- The first amount was used wherever a range is given, such as 3- to 3½-pound whole chicken.
- The first serving number was used wherever a range is given, such as 4 to 6 servings.
- "If desired" ingredients were not included.
- Only the amount of a marinade or frying oil that is absorbed was included.

America's most trusted cookbook is better than ever!

- 1,100 all-new photos, including hundreds of step-by-step images
- More than 1,500 recipes, with hundreds of inspiring variations and creative "mini" recipes for easy cooking ideas
- Brand-new features
- Gorgeous new design

Get the best edition of the *Betty Crocker Cookbook* today!

www.ingramcontent.com/pod-product-compliance
Lightning Source LLC
Chambersburg PA
CBHW071418290426
44108CB00014B/1880